A GIFT ... FOR AN IDIOT

A GIFT ... FOR AN IDIOT

A package of thoughts and poems

By

Dave Dennison

Illustrations and design by

Peter Mair

Original Art by

Mike Cassell

First published in Great Britain
by Directa (UK) Ltd
Cold Norton, Essex. CM3 6UA
2008

©2008 Dave Dennison

ISBN 978-0-9560634-0-3

All Rights Reserved. No part of this publication
may be reproduced, stored in a retrieval system
or transmitted, in any form or by any means,
electronic, mechanical, photocopying, recording
or otherwise, without the prior permission
of the copyright owner.

Printed & Produced
by
Simmons Printers
9 Bilton Road, Chelmsford, Essex

About the Author

Spurs Vice President and entrepreneur Dave Dennison must be multi-faceted! Locally he is known as co-founder of the successful, Essex-based industrial supplies company, Directa, sponsors of the Essex Achievement Awards. However, he is probably more identifiable as a writer, producer, and occasional performer, within the glamorous world of show business.

He co-produced the '1993 outdoor event of the year', twenty-five thousand fans packed inside Hylands Park, Chelmsford to watch, amongst others, chart topping group 'Take That', and American superstar George Benson.
The four days of concerts pre-empted the incredibly popular V Festivals.

In the theatre he worked as co-producer with John Newman on the '97 UK tour of 'Seven Brides for Seven Brothers'. He has worked on many tours including Chas and Dave, Marty Wilde and Joe Brown. His comedy side has led to work with great comedians, like Mike Reid, Bobby Davro and Frank Carson.

He has written stage shows such as 'Over the Rainbow', 'Because You're Mine' and 'All That Jazz'. The highlight of his stage writing was the highly acclaimed musical biography of Mario Lanza, 'The Last Serenade', which toured the UK during 2000 and 2001. His work was recognised by an invitation to become a patron of the Mario Lanza Educational Foundation, joining amongst others José Carreras, and the late tenor Luciano Pavarotti.

He appears regularly, on behalf of charities, as an after dinner speaker, usually billed as Vice President of Tottenham Hotspur Football Club and Russ Abbots' failed scriptwriter! He still finds time to run his businesses as well as writing jokes, sketches, and children's stories... he also found time to write this book!

Yes he is multi-faceted, or he has a secret twin! In any event, Dave's enthusiasm for any new project he takes on knows no bounds, and I know you will thoroughly enjoy this, his latest creation. Life's certainly never dull with D.D around!

PETER G FOOT

Editor *Encore* Entertainment Theatre Magazine

Dedicated to Kathy

who has spent most of her life

dedicated to me

I went to Brooke House School, where, despite being located in the poor East London borough of Hackney, the masters dressed in black gowns more suited to Eton. I left aged fifteen, leaving fourteen year old Alan Sugar behind. We have much in common, we both started out with nothing but poverty. The difference is, I've still got most of mine left!

Multi-millionaire Sir Alan was later to become Chairman of Tottenham Hotspur and me a lowly Vice President. The school has a lot to answer for!

"Wait outside the classroom Dennison" said the offended science master. Once again I'd upset him with a saucy rhyme that made my classmates laugh during the lesson. Afterwards he spoke to me in private, to persuade me not to disrupt his future experiments with daft poems.

"Concentrate more on your science Dennison, you may have a gift for poetry but, **it's a gift for an idiot!"**

A GIFT... FOR AN IDIOT

Here's a book tied up with string
That may not mean anything
Inside is love in large amounts

It's not the thought
But the gift that counts

Thank you for helping to
'spread the love'
by buying this book.

Dave Dennison

Proceeds from the sale of this special edition will go to deserving charities
(Including The Farleigh Hospice and The Alzheimer's Charity at Enfield)

Introduction..................................7

Time To Start By Looking Back 10-11
   The Floor Below.........................12-15
   The Gropers Stroll........................16
   Never Too Old To Rock & Roll 17
   Survival Of The Fittest...................18-23
Time To Take Notice.........................24-25
   Lisa's Pole Position 26
   Human Beans 27
   Pulling Strings..........................28
   Invisible Men 29
   Bound To Happen 30
   Old Shoes 31
   Change Will Do You Good..................32
   Three Feet In A Yard.....................33
Time For A Giggle...........................34-35
   Bin Liner.............................36
   Who's There 37
   A Big One In The Morning 38
   Chinese Whine.........................39
   Best Foot Forward 40-41
   Figure It Out..........................42
   Cremation Tipped.......................43
   Perfect Man..........................44-45

Time To Make It Write 46-47
    Searching For A Setting. 48
    Pour Soul. 49
    Fursdays Efforts 50
    Interact 51
Time To Dilly Dali 52-53
    Waiting For Bermuda 54-55
    Deceptive Majesty 56
    Drop Of A Lid 57
    Rodent Rally 58-59
Time For Holding Hands 60-61
    Empty 62-63
    Percipient 64
    What's Her Name 65
    High Time 66
    Waitress 67
Not A Time For Smiling 68-69
    World Betrayed Centre 70-71
    Too Soon For You To Go .72-73
    Someone Else's Sunday 74
    Fathers Footsteps 75
Time To Say Thank You 76
    Auld Lang Rhyme 77
    Who Needs Drugs 78
    The Floor Below (Song Quiz Answers) 79

What upsets a lot of younger-than-me-folk is that us 'wrinklies' always seem to be going on about the good old days, So I thought it best to get it out of the way early.

I was brought up in what many would think was a less than perfect environment, East London in the fifties. But for me bombsites were not sinister reminders of terrifying air raids, but great adventure playgrounds. I consider myself very fortunate not to have been on the recieving end of those German bombs, and also not to have had to risk my life in defence of my country.

As a boy I experienced amazing music and comedy on Sunday morning radio. Mario Lanza's fantastic voice, Glenn Miller's great orchestra, the Goons, and Round the Horn to name just a few. As a budding teenager I witnessed the birth of Rock and Roll, and as a young 'Mod' the rise of the greatest ever group... The Beatles.

It was a perfect moment in time to enjoy the promiscuous 'swinging sixties', which seemed to have everything, from England winning football's world cup to man stepping on the moon.

Of course it all seems so much better with the passing of time, but as younger readers will discover.....
nostalgia's a thing of the future.

Nostalgia's a thing of the future.

Relax and rest your brain.

Get rid of rear view mirrors,

and don't look back again.

'The Floor Below' was a sixties coffee bar called 'The Pop Inn'. New owner 'Cliff' got the idea of converting the old coal cellar into a moody area without windows, which we thought quite cool, (we used that word then as well). I met both my life long partners there, wife Kathy and business partner Mick. He asked if he could share a go on the pinball table with me using a flipper each, we've had a flipper each ever since!

Slurping espresso, machine going wrong.
A whole lot of shakin,' just a bit too strong.
Jukebox blaring 'Da Do Ron Ron'.
Check out the twist and the loco-motion.
A pretty woman with a sweet talking guy.
It was the place not to walk-on-by.

We'd meet on Saturday at a quarter to three.
Johnny, Paul and Les, but mostly Mick and me.
Not much money, now ain't that a shame,
but plenty of replays on the pinball game.
Smoking Kensitas fags, (coupons to save).
Ain't misbehaving, a long way from the grave.

It was the place to be. It was the place to go.
Next door to 'The Three Crowns', 'The Floor Below'.
Church Street, N. 16. London Town.
Where stupid cupid shot Kathy's clown.
Teenagers in love, seldom singing the blues.
Only crying in the rain for our Hush Puppy shoes.

December '63 the teen beat came.
Something in the air, life will never be the same.
Needles and pins all over your skin.
Mersey beat sounds, the sixties were in.
All the young dudes, wild and free.
All or nothing? You really got me!

He first owned the place, Cliff, a metal guru.
We'd say, no milk today, just a coffee'll do.
"Sugar Sugar?" Cliff would nod.
"Just sweets for my sweet, you silly old sod."
He'd wipe out a cup, looking the part.
Giving jukebox free plays to anyone who had a tart.

Such happy days even better with time.
A new mohair suit, and a gossip of crime.
We would get it on, more than I can say,
take our girls home, then go out to play.
Smooth of face, shaggy of hair.
In a broken car without a care.

All of us were feeling groovy.
Daydream believers like in a movie.
When the time was right,
we'd get around.
Play for the top score,
maybe put on a sound.
Fun, fun, fun, walking like a man.
Working our way back, just to do it again.

Summer in the city, wouldn't that be nice.
Ankle swinging jeans, bumpers half price.
Mellow yellow T-shirts, initialled by pen.
How trendy we were, sunshine supermen.
Wait for the weekend, to be one of a kind.
Monday, Monday, with Friday on the mind.

Yester-me, yester-you, and yester-day.
Our friends didn't leave, they 'had it away'.
Moody geezers, one and all.
All for one, and one for all.
Nowhere to run, nowhere to hide.
Always on each others side.

Then came the Beatles, love me do.
John was me and Paul was you.
What a place to be, what a time we had.
I still feel fine. Can't be bad!

So here's the music from The Floor Below.
From me to you, still making the sixties glow.

Can you find fifty Jukebox Hit titles that appear whole (or in part) in this poem?
One point for title, one for artist, and a bonus point for naming the year!
ANSWERS ON PAGE 79

15

I wrote this following a gift of a musical box that played Love Me Tender. It brought back memories of waiting for the slow song to chat up a girl for a creep (that was a dance). Still... where there's life there's grope !

THE GROPERS STROLL

Elvis was young, Elvis was slim.
Elvis was handsome. Elvis was **in**.

Elvis was cool. Elvis was hip.
Grease on his hair. Curl on his lip.

Elvis sang fast. Elvis could **go**.
But I liked it best, when Elvis sang slow.

'Love Me Tender', that was the chance,
to boldly ask her D'you wanna dance?

If she said yes, blimey what fun.
Left hand on boob, right hand on bum.

Draw her in close, breathe in her ear.
Thigh in her groin, trembling with fear.

Elvis, the King of rock and roll?
Was **Emperor** to us,

The Gropers of Stroll.

16

I was having lunch with ever beautiful singer Susan Maughan. I asked Susan to appear in my show 'Kings and Queens of Rock and Roll'. She agreed saying "Well Dave you're never too old to rock and roll". This bit of nostalgia was given a melody by Chas Hodges and used as the title track for the CHAS AND DAVE album of the same name.

NEVER TOO OLD TO ROCK AND ROLL

Too old to play cowboy games
Too old to remember names
Too old to focus your eyes
Too old to worry 'bout size
Too old to suck your thumb
Too old for bubble gum
Too old to do the splits
Too old to flash your bits
Too old to love all night
Too old for a fairground fight
Too old to grease your hair
(Like to do it but there ain't none there)
Too old for your legs to run
Dad's speed can't catch no one
Too old to touch your toes
Too old to wear tight clothes
But you're never too old...to rock and roll

Old father time will always turn the page
Rock and Roll gets up his nose 'cos it don't seem to age

If you remember coffee bars
What we did in the backs of cars
How we yelled on the waltzer ride
If what you did makes you flush with pride
Then you're never too old to rock and roll

How things have changed? In my boyhood years large well-fed people were rich and thin under fed people were poor. These days it's the other way round!

I attended the annual ball of The Lady Ratling's, as a guest of ventriloquist Roger DeCourcey and his lovely wife, past Queen Ratling, Cheryl. Traditionally the 'Girls' (some of whom are quite mature), stroll around the tables finishing on the dance floor. Then they perform a breathtaking 'Can-Can', each trying to outdo the other's high kicks and splits. Men, a lot younger than me, could only look on in athletic admiration. Perhaps that's why Mae West said
"It's not the men in my life that matter ... It's the life in my men!"

My experience of change and the Ratling program inspired me to put this together.

SURVIVAL OF THE FITTEST

We have survived ! Those of us still around, who were born just before, or not long after the second world war, are the survivors.

We were born before **frozen foods, photocopies, plastics, Polio shots, contact lenses, DVD's, Frisbees** and **the pill.**
Before **credit cards, pin numbers, split atoms, laser beams,** or **ball point pens**. When being **lead-free** just meant a broken pencil.

A time long ago, before **computers**,
when a **P.C.** was a policeman,
hardware was nuts and bolts, and a **damaged disc**
could have you off work for six months.
There was no such word as **software**,
and **microchips** were only available
in bad fish shops.

Long before the orbit of **satellites**,
with only pedal-powered telegrams to keep
us in urgent touch. For us **mobiles** were
simple toys hung above a baby's pram,
and a **text** was only read in Sunday School.

There was no **I.T.** (except in Lyon's Corner House).

It was an age without **fax, digitals**, and **emails**,
when **surfing the net** meant that Mum was cleaning the
curtains and going **on-line** was how she got them dry.

We existed before **tumble dryers, drip dry clothes,
disposable nappies, air conditioners,
electric blankets** and **microwaves**.
In days when a **dish washer** was someone who
shared a bed with a breadwinner.

There were no **househusbands, day care centres,
squatters, dual careers,** or **dating agencies.**
Times when a **meaningful relationship** meant getting
along with the in-laws and **sheltered accommodation**
was where you waited for the bus.
For us **chilling out** simply meant that we'd
forgot to put a vest on.

There was no such thing as **stereophonic radio,** or **digital signals.**
A **DJ** was a black suit and a **CD** was a loaf of bread.
There was no **yoghurt, pot noodles** or **TV dinners.**
We were taught that **fast food** was eaten during lent,
a **big Mac** was a large raincoat

and **crumpet** was something that you ate for tea.

In those days we married first, before we lived together. **Making out** was how we did in exams, a **stud** was how we fastened a collar, **blowjobs** were available at ladies hairdressers, and **going all the way** meant staying on the tram until you reached the depot.

These were times when we thought of **Viagra** as a waterfall in Africa, and being **well-hung** as the ultimate punishment for murderers.

In our day **foreign players** came in a soft packet with a camel's picture. Cigarette smoking was in, but rolling **grass** only happened out in the park. **Coke** was put on the fire, a **joint** was a piece of meat that you had on Sundays, and **pot** was something that you kept under the bed, for emergencies.

For us **rock music** was a grannies lullaby,
and **downloads** only occured when the coalman tipped
the contents of his sack into the coal cellar.
Fergie was a **Ferguson** television set and every housewife
dreamed of owning a twelve inch **Murphy**.

Men who wore earrings were either
pirates or gypsies, and a **gay**
person was nothing, more or
less, than the life and sole of the party.

It was a time when **aids** were no more harmful than
electric ear trumpets.

We have managed to fit in and adapt to changes beyond belief
to be a part of today's world.

We are the fittest and therefore.....

.....**we have survived.**

A man sat relaxing on a bench observing two workmen. One dug a hole and the other immediately filled it in. He watched as a few holes were dug and filled. Eventually he rose from the bench to ask what sort of job they were doing. "We must look silly to you", said the digger, "There's usually three of us but our mate who puts the trees in the holes is off sick today"! Don't you just love 'people watching'?

When I was little and something upset me, my Mum would immediately say 'Take no notice'
I seem to have gone through life doing the absolute opposite!

The great thing about people watching is that we are all so different, each of us having his or her own foibles. By the way foibles (pronounced 'for-balls') means idiosyncrasies, or quirk's. It is a medieval word that describes the weakest point of a sword, (somewhere between the middle of the blade and the point), I suppose that in bygone days, when a Knight was asked why he held a broken sword, he may well have replied "It was foibles!" How frightening!

I detail that description purely for the benefit of those who think foibles is a game of golf played by four golfers.

> You see it your way,
> I see it mine.
> Stand back and look,
> they were twins all the time.

I had the tough job of working on a calendar showcasing some of Peter Stringfellow's beautiful angels. Lisa was one of them and asked if I could write her a poem that could mention the love of her life, Harley.

LISA'S POLE POSITION

Hair brushes your face, pulse's will race.
Lovely bends, subtle curves.
Threaten touch, shifts with swerves.
Lisa, lovely laptop Lisa.
Has so many ways to please you.

Dark darting eyes, promise surprise.
Glossy lipped style, heart breaking smile.
All appears before, but maybe there's more?
Lisa, lovely laptop Lisa.
Has so many ways to tease you.

Why's her skin all aglow? The reason I know,
Lisa's in love. Heavens above!
No chance of romance, just pay for the dance.
Lisa, lovely laptop Lisa.
There is no way to appease her.

From across the room,
Inhale her perfume.
You'll think, maybe yes,
I'll feel her caress.'
But reach for your car key,
Her hugs are for Harley !
Lisa, lovely laptop Lisa.
There is no way for you to seize her.

Harley's the one .... Harley's her son

As a small child I occasionally (rarely) had money to visit 'The Sweet Shop'. There I would agonize for hours to choose the best investment for my thrupenny bit's worth. Flying Saucers, Penny Chews, Fruit Salad, Blackjacks, Sherbet Dabs, Liquorice Twirls, the choice seemed endless. Nowdays all the flavours are available in one type of sweet ...The Jelly Bean.

It made me think that the world has shrunk along with my bag of sweets.

HUMAN BEANS

Some are sweet, some are hot,
some are bright, others not.

Some in stripes, some in plain,
some on top, some down the drain.

Different colours, tastes and shapes,
some like chocolate, some like grapes.

Red, yellow, green and blue,
just like jelly beans, me and you.

Orange, brown, white and pink,
none the same, makes you think.

Plentiful as grains of rice.

Some are bitter,
but
most are nice.

I loved puppets as a child.
I owned a Muffin the Mule marionette which I could just about make walk and nod its head.
Four years old and all that power!

This offering is especially for those who consider themselves important because of their connections.

PULLING STRINGS

If
you
are
a
puppet
it's
handy
to
have
friends
in
high
places

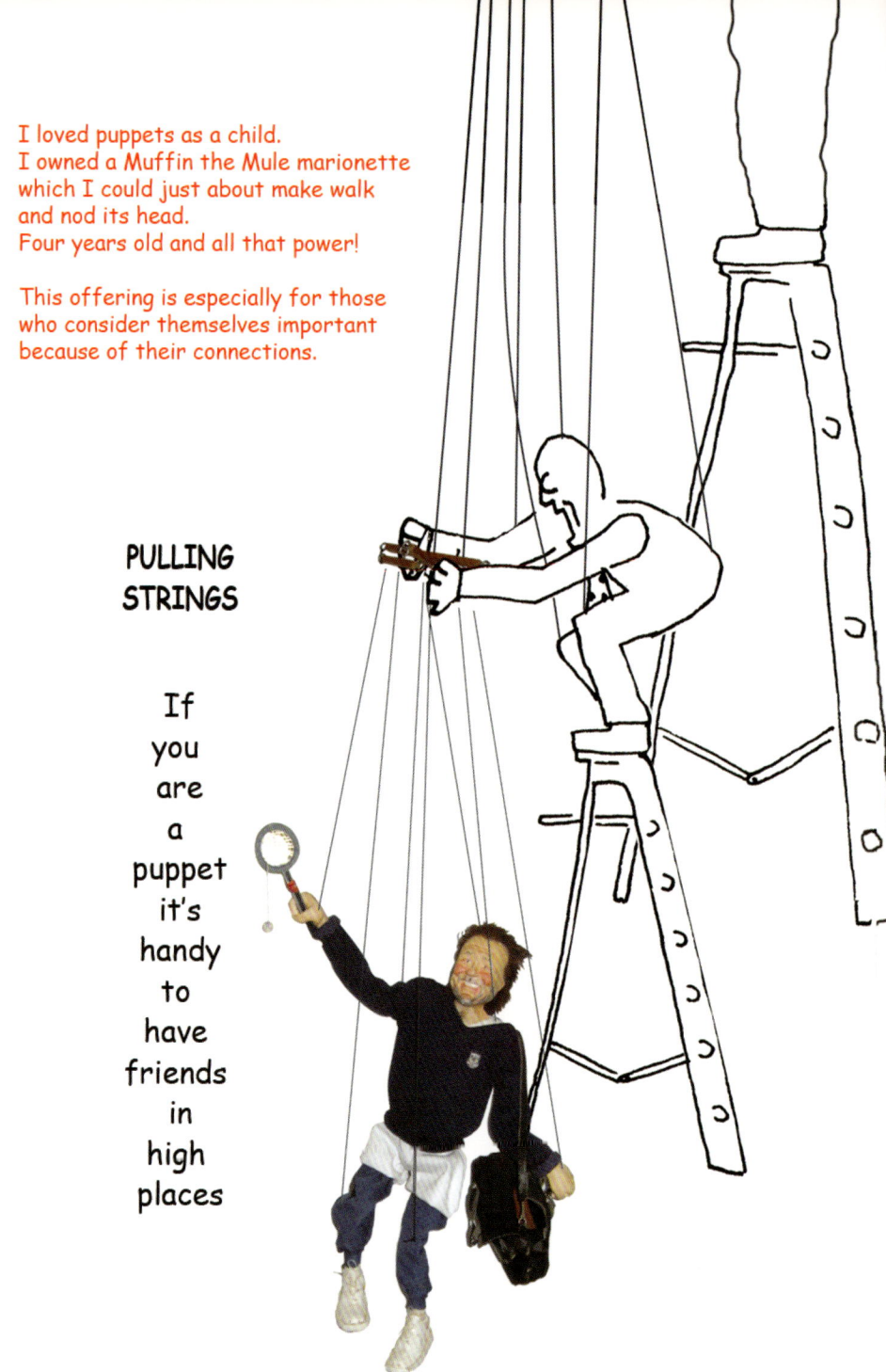

You know the type, big suit, (shoulder pads that could land a helicopter),
loud shirt and flash shoes, boasting of money but never buys a round of drinks.
On a golf course he's the one who drops more names than shots. He likes to
think that he's the centre of attraction, mouthing loudly about some big deal
that will provide the solution to the world economic crisis. Your luck is in, because
he can get you in on the ground floor, all you need to do is invest twenty pounds.
In fact it is a good deal, donate the note and you're unlikely to see him again.

INVISIBLE MEN

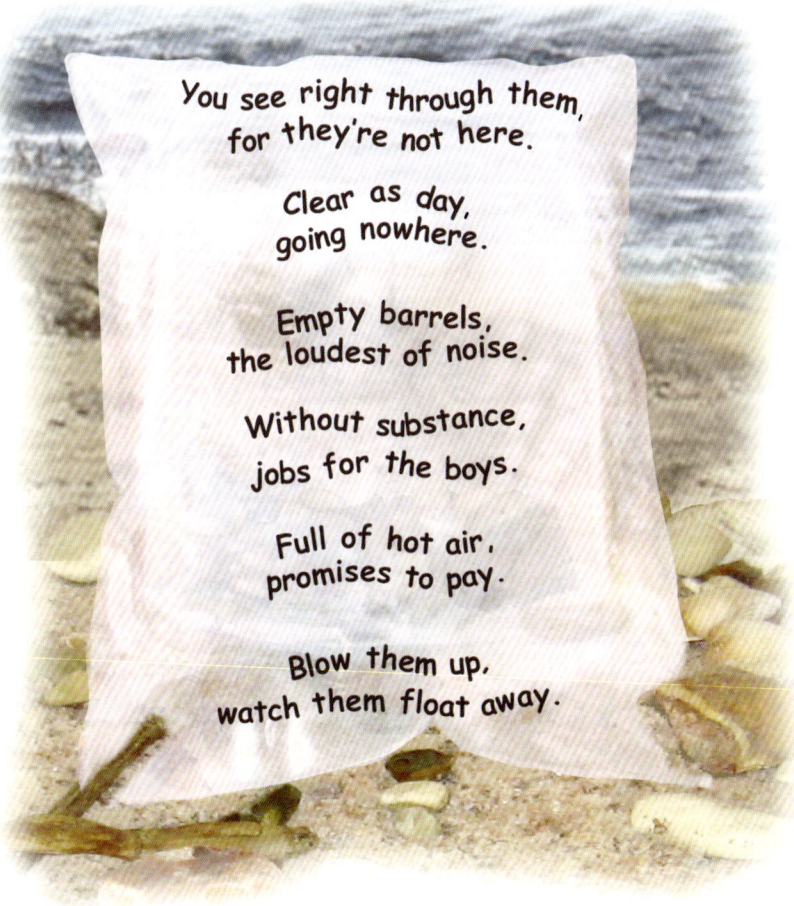

You see right through them,
for they're not here.

Clear as day,
going nowhere.

Empty barrels,
the loudest of noise.

Without substance,
jobs for the boys.

Full of hot air,
promises to pay.

Blow them up,
watch them float away.

They say that 'life's a journey to be savoured' but when you least expect it, a wheel can fall off and cause a depressing halt to even the happiest of passengers. It's then that life itself can seem to be picking on you. Causing frowns and nothing but depressing ruin wherever you look. I believe in the power of positive attitude. Look for the bright side, put a smile on your face and you're back on the road to recovery. For all its faults, life is a gift, and so much better than the alternative.

BOUND TO HAPPEN

The egg,
   how smooth it felt,
      how good it was to look at.
         Perfect, on the outside.
      Crack !
      A line appeared.
   Snap !
      Pieces fell away,
breaking irreparably apart.

All seemed lost, the ruin perfect.

Who would have thought, from such
   wreckage, fresh life could emerge.
      Defying stains of the past,
         progressing forward
            with surprised breath.

The smooth comfort of the egg is missed,
      and the pain remembered.
         But the shell, like its ruin,
     proves temporary.

'The swan is so beautiful,
     how perfectly she glides.'

Look at the pieces of broken shell.

Nothing is perfect ... but there again?

Ah the continuity of life! It's a depressing thought but we all wait in the same queue for the final call. To make matters worse none of us know just how far down the queue we are. Reassuringly, evidence of the everlasting quality of life can be found, it's within those who, through our existence, we have either created or inspired. Grandfather Dennison (who I never met) was a shoe mender by trade. Although his son George (who I called Dad) was a carpenter, he, like his father, would buy odd pieces of leather in the market, place our families shoes on a last and spend part of his Sunday making sure that our feet would stay dry.

Can you imagine a Cobbler arriving at the gates of heaven, presenting the gatekeeper with his entry ticket, only to be told to come back next week!

OLD SHOES

The old cobbler
looked through
the hole in his soul

and thought deeply.

If his youth had last
and hadn't passed,
fine things he would
have done.

Now it's with his son.

For tacks
drop
one,
by
one.

From
withered
dry
lips.

A true primary school story. During an English lesson a small girl asked the meaning of the word 'frugal'. The teacher answered that it meant 'to save'. The closing sentences of the little girl's story read... The Princess was drowning in the lake. She called out to the passing Knight "Frugal me ... please frugal me". He frugalled her and they lived happily ever after I've always tried to be frugal, never too proud to pick up a coin, nor thankfully, to put several in charity tin collections.

CHANGE WILL DO YOU GOOD

How strange
To note the change
As it comes rolling in
Root of all evil
Making the world go round
Will I lose or win?
Fleeing burnt pocket holes
Foolishly it parts
Going as easy as it comes
Breaking miser's hearts

Advice comes cheap
Can you hear?
'Old rope can't buy me love'
The pipers are too dear

Remember only time is money
So be glad
Let time do the talking
But
'Don't waste good time after bad'

Happiness can't buy you money
But
It can take the sting out of poverty

I was on holiday in a deluxe hotel, people watching from a beach bar. In such a situation it's hard not to feel pampered and spoilt. I realised that there were many who quite freely enjoyed the same beach, the same sunshine, and the same waves in which to cool off. In beach wear it's difficult to tell who's local and who's a hotel guest. Even footwear didn't prove a fair test of who's who on the beach. It must annoy some people that the Caribbean is free for all to swim. The sea does not accept reservations at any price. Nature can be a great leveller.

THREE FEET IN A YARD

Three seaside girls
None of them a wife
Three single girls
Three walks of life

Beach bar serving
Miss Waterproof and plain
Comfy working shoes
(Sandals go against the grain)

Passing poor and slipshod
Miss Comb-along-the-beach
While Miss Money in her bare feet
Sips rum through bubbled peach

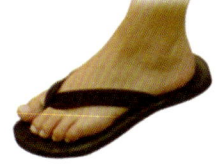

Three different girls
Three sets of jeans
Ripped, torn and worn
Like discarded magazines

Creased up glossy pages
Show what to wear
Upon your feet
But...
It only matters to you
When you've got enough to eat

Flame TV, asked me, in my occasional capacity as a comedy writer and producer, to help with a channel 5 program about comedians, past and present. I was interviewed, live on camera, by a strange looking West Indian gentleman.

Twenty minutes into the proceedings the interviewer shocked me, he raised both his hands and began tearing his face off! There camouflaged beneath a plastic disguise was the great comedian, Mike Reid.

With a little help from prosthetics, expensive clothes and a brilliant Rastafarian wig, he appeared to be a young man, half his age. The real name and nature of the program was 'Age Swap', and I'd been done good and proper.

Some people say that comedy is a serious business ... not me!

Playing golf with Mike (he being a long hitter and me not) he called over and said "Dave I've noticed what you're doing wrong". "What is it Mike?" I said, hoping for a tip or two. "You're standing much too close to the ball" "Am I?" I quizzed. "Yes", he said, "and I mean, after you've hit it!"

A hole or two later he stood motionless, staring in the distance, and again he called to me, this time saying, "Dave look at that". "Look at what?" I said, expecting another joke. "Look at that beautiful landscape, just think how lucky we are to be here. ... never take it for granted."

Mike has departed now for stages and golf clubs anew, but I wont forget his advice.

Here's a little 'anon' poem that never ceases to make me smile.

I'm a little glow-worm
I am never glum
How can I be miserable
When the sun shines out my bum

35

I loved the humour of Tommy Cooper. My mate Russ Abbott's great stage impression 'Cooperman' would often include this little poem written either by Russ or someone by the name of A.Nonymous.

As I went walking with my brother Jim
Somebody threw a tomato at him
Tomatoes are soft and they don't hurt the skin
But this one did... it came in a tin!

I also like this old poem which could have been written by Mr. Nonimous especially for Tommy.

I eat my peas with honey
I've done it all my life
It makes the peas taste funny
But it keeps them on the knife

Here's one I penned
with the great man in mind.

BIN LINER

Today I wrote a poem

I wrote it in a hurry

It was full of gloom and woe

I tore it up don't worry!

*I originally wrote this for children to help them not to be afraid of the dark.
Its turned the light on for a few of them, hopefully it'll do the same for you!*

WHO'S THERE ?

He's tall ....He's short
He's thin ....He's fat
He's here ....He's there
He's where ....You're at
Staring ....Sneering
Ready.........................To pounce
Gobble ....You up
Ounce............................By ounce
There's.......................No escape
You...............................Can find
The Monster................You see
Is in...........................Your mind.

*If your fear still lingers
Try squinting up your eyes
And peeping
Through your fingers*

37

Famed for her outrageous innuendo's and double-entendre, cockney beauty Denise van Outen (a big fan of Chas and Dave) was the star of TVs 'Big Breakfast Show'. I wrote this in '98 as the lyric for a cheeky theme song for her and the show. Chas and Dave put some great music to it but alas she never got to record the song as she left to join the cast of 'Chicago' to become a big West End star.

A BIG ONE IN THE MORNING

There's nothing stops me yawning,
like a big one in the morning.

Bacon, eggs, wiv a sausage on the side.
English breakfast, full of pride.
First I get to feel real loose,
knocking back me orange juice.
Then I lose all me aches,
wiv a bowl of tasty flakes.
Tea steaming in me cup.
Both me eggs sunny side up.
Loads an loads of crispy bacon,
sure to stop me belly achin'.
Open me mouth extra wide,
'arf a marta' takes a ride.
Then the fing that I like mosta,
as I lift a slice from the toaster,
watchin' breakfast on the Telly,
bunging toast an marmers down me belly.
You can keep you fruit an muesli,
only big ones can amuse me.

There's nothing stops me yawning,
like a big one in the morning.

Don't know about you but I love Chinese food. To help me digest I rub Bhudda's belly ... then mine! Apologies to all my Chinese friends .... after a few glasses I get Rs over L bowed !

CHINESE WHINE

Pick at bits you rike the most,
Flied seaweed, plawn on toast.
Chopstick game, pancake stab,
Hard spling loll, soft shell clab.
King Plawn, special flied lice,
Peanut satay, velly nice.
Sizzring steak, swee 'n sour,
Plenny dishes by the 'our.
Rot of stuffin' to survive.
Confucious he say,
'Duck and Dive'.
Margalitas,
Not sip slow.
Many grass,
Flench Merot.
Coffee, Blandy,
Feering fine.
Double portion ..... Sixty Nine!

Peter Mair takes the blame for this. He plonked a strange pair of tartan boots on my desk. He'd used them for a publicity photo for Chas and Dave's poster of their tour of Scotland. "Surely you can write something about these?" he said.

The result might be a little corny but I like it.

BEST FOOT FORWARD

Walking home, in running shoes,
I get the lace-up, casual blues.
I've forced my feet into winkle-pickers,
Doctor Martins, sweaty kickers,
chisel toed with metal tips,
Chelsea boots with Hackney zips.
Beetle crushers, brothel creepers,
heavy as two railway sleepers.
Welly boots, that don't quite fit,
summer sandals, full of grit.
Sling back strap, like Kylie Minogues,
dodgy crepe, and Irish brogues.
Patent leather, buckle over,
Velcro fasten, Alligator,
Dunlop flash, Netherland clogs,
Loafers (as worn by the Troggs).
Noddies' platforms beneath my socks,
just like standing on a box.
Desert boots with waterproof soles,
worn-out trainers, full of holes.
Bumpers at nine bob a pair,
Moon boots loomed in Yeti hair.

Golfing shoes, with a hole in one.
Flip without flop, singular fun.
Lonely Cuban heel, worn through,
can't do the two-step with just one shoe !

This foot long list is never ending
yet
none of them......were worth the mending.

FOOTNOTE

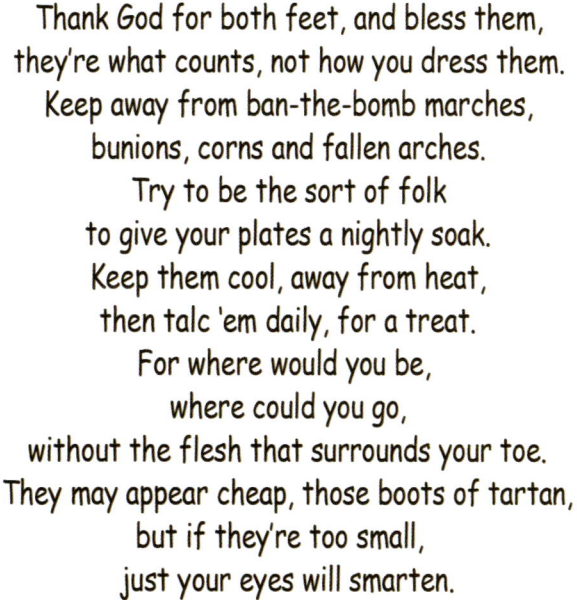

Thank God for both feet, and bless them,
they're what counts, not how you dress them.
Keep away from ban-the-bomb marches,
bunions, corns and fallen arches.
Try to be the sort of folk
to give your plates a nightly soak.
Keep them cool, away from heat,
then talc 'em daily, for a treat.
For where would you be,
where could you go,
without the flesh that surrounds your toe.
They may appear cheap, those boots of tartan,
but if they're too small,
just your eyes will smarten.

A shoe-size dropped can be the worst,
don't be too tight... **put your feet first.**

I was asked to propose the toast for lovely President's Lady Karen Duce. The function coincided with International Women's Day. I.W.D was one of my inspirations in this composition, her husband Gary was the other.

FIGURE IT OUT

The battle of the sexes is so old in the tooth.
I once applied science to discover the proof.
Why, when you ask of marriage, who is superior?
Women answer first,
'men are inferior.'
Mind you,
you don't need to be a Steven Hawking
to hear men come second,
(when it comes to talking).

I tried using simultaneous equations,
to check for the difference
in marital relations.
I thought with mathematics,
my case can be won.
Surely a half plus a half
just adds up to one.
I'd believed marriage was
50/50 actions.
But I proved, I didn't understand women,
and I didn't understand fractions.

I now accept, men walk,
upon a different path,
and I give thanks that
'equal partnerships',
means we've got a better half.

Marlboro cigarettes may have killed more cowboys than the Indians, but there are still those who can't give up the dreaded weed. It's a drag in more ways than one. 'Cremation Tipped' is dedicated to smokers everywhere who would like to give up before it's too late.

CREMATION TIPPED

AN APPLE A DAY
KEEPS THE DOCTOR AWAY

A DRAG A DAY
WILL HELP ME TO PLAY

A FAG A DAY
WILL SOOTHE THE WAY

A COUPLE A DAY
IS DOUBLY OKAY

A PACKET A DAY
DON'T HURT YOUR PAY

FIFTY A DAY
BUT I THROW HALF AWAY

SMOKE WHAT I LIKE A DAY
SOD THE DECAY

LAST BURN UP TODAY
I'M IN THE ASHTRAY

43

For all those men who have made the mistake of forgetting a wedding anniversary or buying the wrong birthday gift. Mind you I still can't see what was so wrong about a pair of Tottenham Hotspur Pyjamas, apart from the size. So here at last, is the perfect reply for us much criticised males.

HER PERFECT MAN

"What's wrong with you," I said,
(she'd moaned about making the tea)
"I want a perfect man," she groaned.

I said "So how's he different from me?"

"The perfect man is gentle," she said,
"He's never unkind or mean.
He has a beautiful smile,
And keeps his face so clean".

"The perfect man likes children" she said,
"And he'll raise them by your side.
He'll offer to take care of them,
 Giving time off to his bride".

"The perfect man loves cooking" she said,
"Washing and ironing too.
He'll arrange a vase of flowers,
To show his love for you".

"The perfect man
is sensitive"
she said.
"Writing poetry in your name.
He's a best friend
to your mother
And kisses away your pain".

"The perfect man
loves to shop"
she said,
"He'll go with you every day".

I said

"I've got news for you
my dear

The perfect man is gay!"

words•worth

Time to
make it write

I suppose I've always been interested in playing with words.
It must have been something that I inherited from my Mother.
I remember asking her what the word 'syllables' meant,
she said it was something she called my Father.

It seems that almost every English word has an alternative
meaning or another word that sounds just like it.
How any foreign speaker can grasp the finer points of our
language is beyond me. For instance how do you explain
'Jumping on a bus', 'Hopping in the bath' or 'Sailing into a room'?

A tiny friend of mine once told me a joke.

"What's the difference between a soldier and a fireman?"
I gave up (as you do) and asked what the difference was.
"Well silly"
I could tell he was enjoying having one over his elders
(If you pardon the expression)
" You can't dip a soldier in your egg!"

What a great language we all share!

Why do poets starve

when they can coin a phrase

worth noting?

h

OOPS dropped an H

47

Writers block can spark off some unusual offerings. Staring at a blank sheet of paper with one eye on an Olympic high-board diving event and ……

SEARCHING FOR A SETTING

On high
look below
deep breath
here we go

Diving from a silent raft

Slow motion
plunging
jack knife
lunging

Deep down dictionaries shaft

Full stop
I splash upon
a bed of letters

Exploding words
confetti above

Like Diamonds
(Like Love)

SEARCHING FOR A SETTING

On each occasion that I've wandered into my study the worse for drink, I have produced a work of art. However the next morning an evil noise rips through my fragile hung-over brain. It's the sound of the 'masterpiece' being torn before I file under R, in the bin. A friend once said to me you'd be better off drinking the ink ... at least it could make you write!
Right or wrong this 'Pour Soul' escaped the bin.

POUR SOUL

next to the drink
stands
the ink

lubricate
to
communicate

after the port
stands
the thought

how close to the rim
stands
the rhyme

how near to
the verse
stands
the Universe

are words
simply
worlds
without the
L plates

Ann baked a special cake for Kelly's fortieth birthday. Unlike husband Mick, Kelly never ever used bad language. Therein came the idea for Kelly's F-word birthday, why not an F-word cake to depict the second F-word to be banned in their house ...FORTY! The large F shaped cake sported forty little flags each with its own to be banned f-word. I did a little F- word speech at the party which climaxed with the entry of the cake. I baked this with the left over F-Words.

FURSDAYS EFFORT   (A flagrant breach of the peace)

Furiously fed-up fight fans frowned
Whilst fearless flower fondlers
Fingered fractured fairy cakes
A FRAGRANT BREACH OF THE PIECE

Fourteen fair flaxen floozies flaunted
Five fiery flambé fingers
Fried in fatty fashion
A FERVENT REACH OF THE GREASE

Fortune reading fairground fakers
Fleeced family female of fifteen
For fancy flat at Frinton-on-Foam
A FAKIR RENT BEACH OF THE NEICE

Four fully fledged French fishermen
Foisted friendly feelings by
Fondly flying a Finnish flag
A FLAGWRENCH BRANCH OF THE PEACE

Few forest fruits forgive
Frantic factory farmers
Fornicating ferociously
A FARM BENT BESEECH OF THE PEAS

Fifty foolish federal fellows
Framed forty four felons for
Forgetting to fasten flies
AN F.B.I. PIECE OF THE BREECHES

Scientist Isaac Newton's law stated that for every force there's an equal and opposite force. It's interesting to note that when you rhythmically put down a batch of words that scan and rhyme, they often refer to and seem to need each other. Just like people I suppose.

INTERACT

Whiskey Mac - Armagnac - Fast Food Snack - Heart Attack

Cadillac – Double Back – Bric-a-Brac – Money Back

Chimney Stack – Santa's Sack – Pak-a-Mac – Got the Sack

Caddy Shack – Paddy Whack – Frere Jacques – Fleet Street Hack

Power Pack – Got the Knack – Alice Slack - Front to Back

Change of Tack – Champagne Rack - Billy Mac - Shuffled Pack

Carpet Tack – Dirty Crack - Dental Plaque – Lustre Lack

Jumping Jack – Railroad Track - Donald Quack – Shark Attack

Shoulder Pack – Clothing Rack - Jumbo Pack - Broken Back

Almanac - Crinkle Back – Grannies Shack - No Way Back

CD track - Jimmy Mack – Shackatack - Cilla Black

Wake up Jack – Playful Smack – Crackerjack - Don't Look Back

Coming Back - Lumber Jack - Long Lost Track - Don't Turn Back

Tic-a-Tac - Vacumac - Celeriac - Grocer Jack

Bergerac - Too Laid Back - Dog called Zak – No Feedback

Back to Back – Sticky Back – Black is Black -That's a fact

Apple Mac -Torture Rack - Go get packed! .....yak – yak – yak

51

Time to dilly Dali

My appreciation of the work of Salvador Dali began in 1970.

A very tall and Broad Californian entered the menswear shop that I was getting ready to open in London's Villiers Street, together with my partners Mick and Terry. The shop's name 'Mr. Toad' caught the eye of red haired American Mike Cassell. He asked if he could paint the shop front, only receiving payment if we were happy with his work. It turned out that this likeable and unique individual was a talented artist, you'll find some examples of his work reproduced in this book. He lived in London where he worked at the night club 'Maximus' as a doorman, wearing the clothes of a Roman Centurian. We became great friends, and it was he who introduced me to surrealism and Dali.

One of Dali's famous explanations of his surreal art was to describe the 'virtual' cup.

He suggested sticking a teaspoon on a saucer at an angle of roughly 45 degrees. Stare at it long enough and you will be able to see the missing cup, courtesy of your imagination of course.

Mike opened my eyes to seeing things differently and encouraged me to write with imagination.

**To paint a picture
you need paint and encouragement
in that order**

**Too many people suffer
from encouragement
but no paint**

I loaned artist Mike Cassell his air fare to return home to California. He sent me an oil painting in payment; with it a note challenging me to illustrate the surreal picture with words. He had already titled the canvas 'Waiting for Bermuda'. Later the painting was accepted for exhibition at The East London Arts Festival, where it proudly hung between a David Hockney and a sketch by sculptor Henry Moore. Mike also entered the framed poem for display with the painting. The poem was refused as it contradicted the hanging rules; He then entered it, on its own, without my knowledge, in the poetry section. Coincidentally, as President of the local chamber of commerce, I received an invitation to attend the poetry competition awards evening. Very prestigious for Hackney, attended by, amongst others, BBC radio and the then Prime Minister's wife Mary Wilson. I slipped out ten minutes before the end, and unbeknown to me missed my poem being read out by the late Poet Laureate John Betjeman, as runner up.

'Waiting for Bermuda'   Oil on canvas by Mike Cassell

WAITING FOR BERMUDA

Black
Shiny sky
Cries on a barracuda
She lies
Trying to die
Like a long lost ... loser
At last
Her sand - ran dry
Waiting for Bermuda

Sky
Made of seaweed

Waves
Made of cloud

Body
Made mortal

Silence
Made loud

Another of Mike's surreal works, this time in pencil, prompted me to give it a title and write this barbed comment on how some of the superior sex deal with unrequited passion.

DECEPTIVE MAJESTY

Place the void in camouflage
Veneer with Khaki-drapes
Hide a sneer
in eyes too large
Piercing cut glass flakes
Untouchable ... secret gloom
Impression leaves all
to chance
Feline grace
perfumes the room
in stillness
she appears to dance
She'll rise
yet fall
to every call
from tight lipped
lusty slaves
Each one will try
to penetrate
her sensual
tide-less waves

My fire is dim
self comforting
Penetration once was mine
Then satisfaction
sucked from me
Her Majesty spat out my mind

56

Written after a strange dream, which appeared to predict the events of the following day.

THE DROP OF A LID

Somewhere between
Wide asleep and deep awake
Lay my dormant dream

Returning from the past
Half remembered handshakes
Enact bizarre fantasies
Watched by the grinning face of tomorrow

Identities
Speeding to and fro
Shielded from my curiosity
By uninformed memory

Emotions
Pleasing, scaring
Indeed
Even the ability to fly is mine
At the drop of a lid

Enormous strength
Puny weakness
Reach out!
Grasp at an image
It turns to water
My hand emerges dry

Yet somehow I have touched the future

A Rolls Royce stopped by a scruffy man at the kerbside. The chauffeur lowered the blacked-in rear window. The passenger spoke to the vagrant. "Aren't you Sydney Rubenstein? It's me Alan Sweetener, we were friends at school? What in heaven's name has happened to you?"
"I'm down on my luck", Rubenstein replied sadly.
"Business went broke, wife left me, and the bank took away my house."
"I am very successful in business", bragged Sweetener . "Is there anything I can do to help?"
"Well I could do with ten pounds for a bed."
"Bring it round in the morning," said Sweetener, "I'll have my buyer take a look at it."

Many a true word said in jest. Three things helped me compose Rodent Rally, my Romany blood, a frustrating day at the office and artist Mike Cassells laid back attitude to life.

RODENT RALLY

Gypsy use your crystal ball
Foretell by Tarot charm
Will my lot be big or small?
Read this outstretched palm
Can you tell me wise Romany
How to satisfy my life?
Why is it I don't seem to be
Fulfilled with all this strife?
I try so hard to lead the pack
To point my nose in front
I compete each day with greedy rats
In this race am I also one?

"Fortune's in your hands my friend"
He said with sage like grin
"In your race there is no end
Ambition's a forever thing
Why not relax, enjoy the day
Fear not of future plans
Distant sky may change from grey
You could become a contented man
Take my advice, invest in life
It's a priceless gift bestowed
Don't give your love ... but loan it all

Think what a wealth you'll be owed"

Time for holding hands

Once I had a secret love ....

It was for beer-swilling, gun-slinging, buckskin-covered ladette cowgirl, Calamity Jane. Her love for cowboy Wild Bill Hickok enabled her to transform into beautifully feminine Doris Day. Yards of frills, petticoats and gingham, were involved (perhaps a bit of make up as well).
How I dreamt of holding her hand as I sat staring open mouthed at the silver screen.

Romance had begun for me a few years earlier as I watched Bambi meet his Doe with the long eyelashes.
Wow, I thought, that's worth giving up Thumper for!

I am still just as soppy as I was then, regularly weeping at films such as 'Ghost' or 'Sleepless in Seatle'.

Real life can be just as exciting and heart wrenching if you let it.

My personal romance has been going on much longer than I care to admit, yet it can still surprise me as much as it did Bambi and Bill.

Vin is French for wine

Age is an attitude of mind

T is for two

Me is for you

Put them together

Best vintage ever!

Just hearing the word 'empty' conjures up an image of an empty bottle with a money back deposit. As a boy I would hunt empties with a passion, sometimes retrieving them from the yard of a pub and taking them round the front for my pocket money! These days we consider recycling as something modern. We carefully place our washed bottles in the council's special container for fortnightly collection. The bottles are then colour separated by hand, shipped miles away for crushing, then shipped further miles away for melting, until restored to the shape of a bottle, they travel to be filled with liquid, until finally (after even more travel) they end up once again on the supermarket shelves. Perhaps our old system wasn't so bad after all.

We can all occasionally take the past for granted, as we can also accidently do with our partners. This poem sums up the need for a home to be more than possessions.

EMPTY

empty as
an open cage
a cell without a lock
as empty as
marble echoes'
that tick upon the clock

empty as
a railway track
rusting low in wind-sown weeds
as empty as
a ghost town bench
yesterday's film set bleeds

empty as
a dead man's bowl
like a sunday in the city
as empty as
a warden's heart
a ticket with no pity

empty as
a playground swing
with no children playing
as empty as
an alpine school
without a snowflake laying

empty as
a desert
bereft of any sand
like a pub with no happy hour
a gig without a band

empty as
the vacuum
within a liars promise
the conscience
of a new born babe
trustingly still honest

as empty as
my vacant stare
when I'm really blue
but nothing...no-thing
is as empty

as our home is... without you.

"I knew you was going to say that." How many times have you heard that phrase or said it yourself to someone close. It's all about understanding without words. A 'Percipient' communicates without words just like a teardrop!

PERCIPIENT

A drip
A drop
A moist shiny drip
Insignificant
Almost irrelevent
Yet
Placed upon your cheek
It proved you cared

Original watercolour   by Peter Mair

Despite Shakespeare's advice that 'a rose by any other name would smell as sweet' we still get into a state of panic trying to choose suitable names, particularly for girls. There was the case of the American millionaire, Mr. Rose, who wanted his first born girl to have a beautiful and unusual name. He chose to call her Wilde. The trouble was that when grown up Wilde Rose married Mr. Bull !

WHAT'S HER NAME

What will they call this child, '**Pure**', like driven snow?
She must have identity, a name to put on show.
Simply she is '**Happiness**', for she has brought it here.
Or otherwise '**Contentment**', for she has banished fear.
An apt name would be '**Magnet**', for we can't keep away.
Or better still '**Miss Sunrise**', the beauty of the day.
Royally she'd be '**Princess**', for she is fair to all.
Equally she is '**Majesty**', surely born to rule.
With a name like '**Permission**', she'd always have her way.
But if she's called '**Nutrition**', she'd get bigger every day!
Her name should be '**Innocence**', for that is all she knows.
It could be '**Perfection**', see her fingers and her toes.
Perhaps we'll call her '**Pride**', as in all of us she swells.
One day it will be '**Bride**',
the prettiest of girls.
Maybe we'll name her '**Wonder**',
for she is wonderful.
A cute name could be '**Total**',
to her family she is all.
We have no name to call
her yet, but maybe,
in the meantime we will
call her '**Love**',
the best name for our baby.

Written March 23rd 1993 Amy's Birthday. (Amy derived from Latin, meaning greatly loved.)

65

Two heads may be better than one but hold the hand of someone special and you'll experience more ups and downs than Superman's cape in a lift!

HIGH TIME

The hand upon my watch
will stop,
if I fail to wind.
The intimate parts of
my high
will drop,
if I fail to find.
The one that holds my hand,
does so because she understands,
the height of my high,
and the depths of
my low.

I can soar above,
I can dive
below.

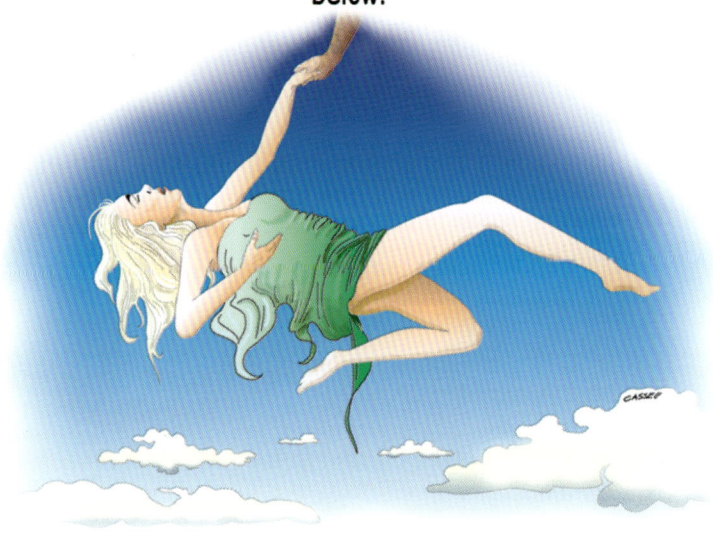

American friend and artist Mike Cassell suffered acute lust at first sight in a local restaurant. He asked me to write some romantic lines to help break the ice. Apparently the poem did the trick and neither of them wasted any more time waiting!

WAITRESS

Her eyes were so blue,
you could swim right through,
yet, black, silky hair,
defied the paleness
of her origins.
Neat proportions
swathed in white,
revealed themselves,
when backed by light.
Teeth to put a dentist
on the dole.
Surrounded by lips,
built to caress
and console.

She approached as if
under Scrutiny
with a plate of shish-kebab,
chips and tea.

Not a time for smiling

Sometimes I have written about events that are sad, and occasionally sombre. It has always been an unenjoyable task, yet I have often found a release, and a way to find direction with a new place to begin.

Some believe black to be the dullest of all colours.
I wonder whether white would seem as bright without it?

Grief

is a blotch.

It spills upon us

when we least expect it..

Tears, time and friendship.

Nature's,

heaven sent,

stain removers.

WORLD BETRAYED CENTRE

London was low 'n down
Brussels bristled in disbelief
Geneva couldn't believe either
Dubai began to cry
Oslo had never been so low
Copenhagen couldn't cope
Helsinki sank
Madrid went mad
Paris lost its kiss
Cologne was spent
Glasgow full of woe
Dublin doubled up in pain
Belfast slowed to a crawl
Derry no longer merry
Tel Aviv continued to grieve
Melbourne began to mourn
Perth could not be worse
Taipei cried all day
Saigon went missing
Stockholm suffered at home

Berlin stayed in
Rome would not roam
Vancouver a non-mover
The Samba stopped in Rio
Frisco closed the disco
Las Vegas was lost
Chicago saw its star go
San Diego saw the day go
Salt Lake filled with tears
The States United in sorrow

The insane lit fires of hatred
Kabul bellowed bull
Islamabad just as bad
Palestine anything but pally

Nairobi to Sierra Leone
Africa wept but not alone
Across the world City to City
the good sat wrenching hands in pity

Heaven heaved a sigh

New York was not new anymore

The family had gathered in Eastbourne, young and old alike, to celebrate the lives of my lovely in-laws Mill and Bill. Tragically they had passed away a year earlier. Surprisingly Bill first, then a few weeks later Millie finally escaped Alzheimer's disease. The Saturday visit to 'Seven Brides for Seven Brothers' and an Italian meal had cheered everyone. The following morning I turned on the Hotel TV and learned of Princess Diana's terrible accident. I wrote 'Too Soon' shortly after. I have used it as part of the eulogy to my late business partner Bob, as well as reading it to the members of the Mario Lanza appreciation society. The title alone makes it meaningful to all of us who have suffered a loss, be it directly or indirectly.

TOO SOON FOR YOU TO GO

I don't know why whiskey doesn't freeze,
Or what's so special about a bees two knees.
I don't know why a bubbles round,
Or why a battle lost, can't be found.
I don't know why greens make you curly,
Or why heavens gates should be pearly.
What good is red steak on a black eye,
Or why it is a penguin can't fly.
Why carrots help us to see in the dark,
Or why we leave our cars in a park.
I don't know why black folk sing the better blues,
Or what's so smart about a crocodile's shoes.
I don't know how to win the pools,
Or what sort of gold is meant just for fools.

How can a square dance be so modern?
Or why it is, new cement can't be trod on.
I don't know why the grass is green,
And I can't tell butter from margarine.
I don't know why an eye needs a bath,
Or why you have to be good, for a laugh.
I don't know how a jury can be hung,
Or why it is the good die young.
I don't know why lovers have to part.
Or, how to live with a broken heart.
Why does a night alone, take twice as long?
Why don't you know what you've got, until it's gone?
I don't know why life lets me down,
And I don't know why you're not around.
There's just one thing for sure I know,

It was much too soon for you to go.

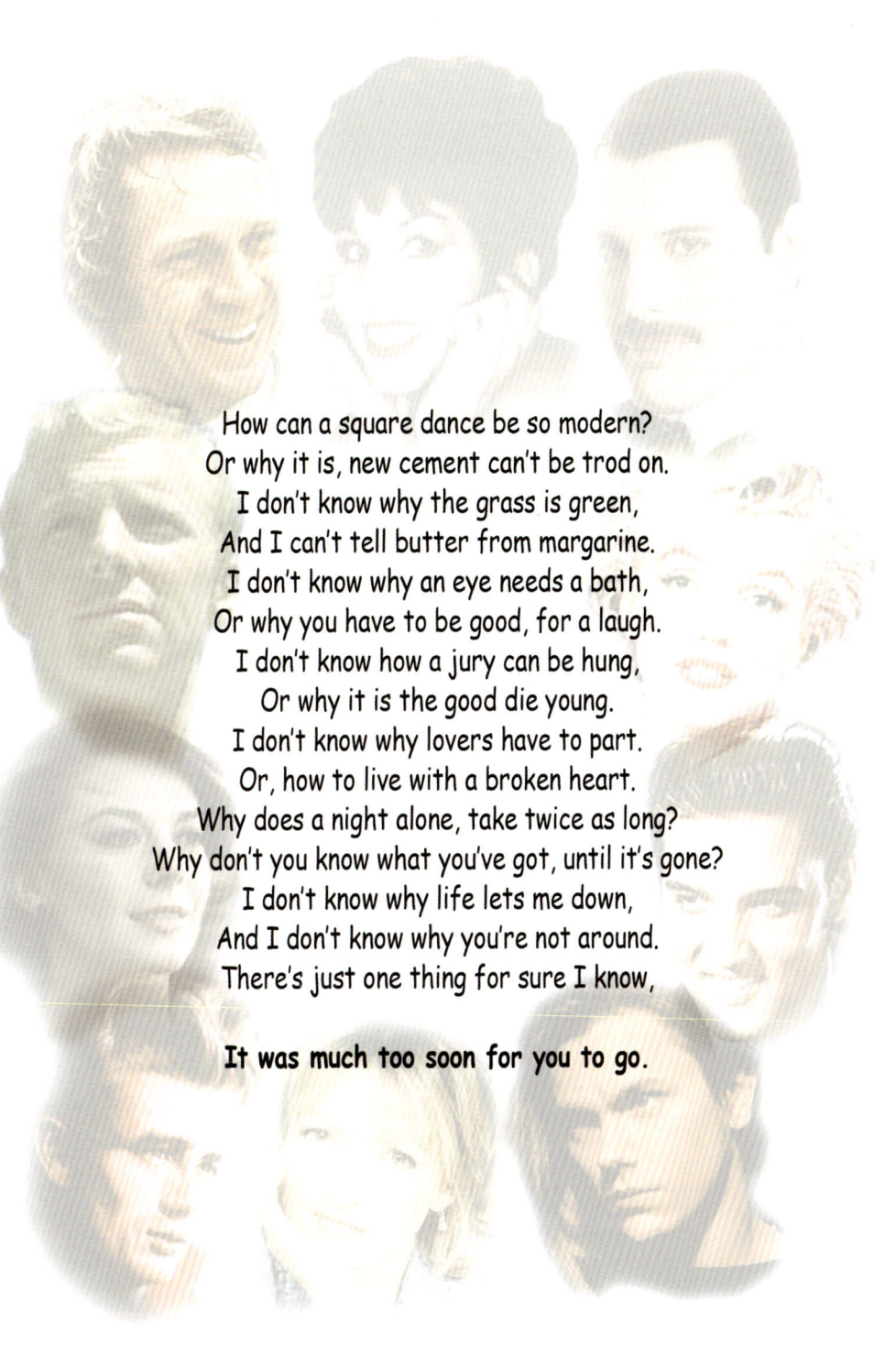

My dearest friend had been a father to his, long awaited, adopted son for only a short time, when events overtook him and left him no choice but to end his ten year marriage. Sunday visits upset everybody. I wrote this for him after he tearfully told me that he had decided to no longer visit his son.

SOMEONE ELSES SUNDAY

If I were blind,
I could still hear your joy.
If I were deaf,
I could still watch my growing boy.

To be apart shows no visible pain.
Just a hollow sickness ... I won't see you again.

If I were selfish,
thinking just of me,
then every Sunday we could go to tea.
I could invent some believable tale,
but never, ever, could I tell you how.
This strange world tricked me,
took me in,
forced my decision,
to begin once again.

Just for you I must stay away.
so you can be part
of someone else's Sunday.

This dip in my past, was at one time turned into a song by singer Steve Cockburn, who I helped get on to TVs 'New Faces', a forerunner of Pop Idol. It was always well received by audiences, but unfortunately he wasn't.

FATHERS FOOTSTEPS

A well-measured balance toe-after-toe,
left leg to follow where right must go.
Gingerly forward step-after-step,
I have never fallen least not till yet.

Fathers footsteps paved the way.
His noisy footsteps paved the way.
Though I was young, there was no time to play,
when fathers footsteps walked away.

Years of careful practice one-after-one,
totally wasted father like son.
Fate nudged my shoulder bye-after-bye,
now the tightrope walker must learn to fly.

Fathers footsteps paved the way.
His noisy footsteps paved the way.
Though I was young, there was no time to play,
when fathers footsteps walked away.

Time to say thank you

To those worthy charities, thanks for all the good work that you do and for providing me with a reason to publish. If you bought this book to give as a present, thank you. If you received it as a present but would have preferred something made of chocolate, sorry, but at least books are calorie free. If you have persuaded a friend to buy a copy, thanks. If you are that friend thanks for being a good one! Keep spreading the word and we'll keep selling the book, continuing to spread the love.

To all those lovely people that I've driven half crazy during the creative, production and sales processes, a big THANK YOU.

Thanks to the lovely Nicky for all her proof reading, again and again and again.

Finally, special thanks to my pal Peter Mair for his excellent design work, nagging and encouragement. He's not a bad bloke for an Arsenal fan!.

Dave xo

THE END ... What a terrible pair of words? I prefer instead to view 'the end' as THE BEGINNING. 'Tomorrow is the first day of the rest of your life', I wish I'd composed that phrase. For those dismal Jimmy's who counter with, 'What if I'm not here'? Well then, tomorrow may be the first day for you to discover the secrets of the universe, either way it's a beginning. As a parting gift I leave you with my New Years poem together with my thanks for sharing the thoughts of an idiot!

AULD LANGS RHYME

A New Year
A clean page
Props gone
An empty stage
An ink dipped pen
Awaiting pressure
The New Year
Love
Life
and
Leisure

If you've reached this far, you've travelled past 'the end' to look for a new beginning...well done.

I hope you've enjoyed my company...thank you for being the instrument of my music...and thanks for the dance.

Who needs drugs
or other bugs.
No need to try
when music
makes you high.

The Floor Below Pop Quiz ...ANSWERS

These songs helped inspire the poem.
Here are the titles, in full, in the order they appear.

Whole Lot of Shakin' Goin' on	Jerry Lee Lewis	1957
Da Doo Ron Ron	Crystals	1963
The Twist	Chubby Checker	1960
The Loco-Motion	Little Eva	1962
Oh Pretty Woman	Roy Orbison	1964
Sweet Talkin' Guy	Chiffons	1966
Walk on by	Dionne Warwick	1964
Quarter to three	Gary US Bonds	1961
Money	Bern Elliot & the Fenmen	1963
Ain't that a shame	Fats Domino	1957
Ain't Misbehavin'	Tommy Bruce & the Bruisers	1960
Stupid Cupid	Connie Francis	1958
Cathy's Clown	Everly Bothers	1960
A Teenager in Love	Marty Wilde	1959
Singing the Blues	Tommy Steele	1956
Cryin' in the Rain	Everly Brothers	1962
December '63 (Oh What a Night)	Four Seasons	1976
Teen beat	Sandy Nelson	1959
Something in the air	Thunderclap Newman	1969
Needles and Pins	Searchers	1964
All the Young Dudes	Mott the Hoople	1972
All or Nothing	Small Faces	1966
You really got me	The Kinks	1964
Metal Guru	T-Rex	1972
No Milk Today	Herman's Hermits	1966
Sugar Sugar	The Archies	1969
Sweets for my Sweet	The Searchers	1963
Wipe Out	The Surfaris	1963
Anyone who had a heart	Cilla Black	1964
Get it on	T-Rex	1971
More Than I Can Say	Bobby Vee	1961
59th St. Bridge Song (Feeling Groovy)	Harpers Bizarre	1967
Daydream Believer	Monkees	1967
I Get Around	Beach Boys	1964
Fun, Fun, Fun	Beach Boys	1962
Walk like a Man	Four Seasons	1963
Workin' my way back to you	Four Seasons	1966
Do it Again	Beach Boys	1968
Summer in the City	Lovin' Spoonful	1966
Wouldn't it be nice	Beach Boys	1990
Mellow Yellow	Donovan	1967
Sunshine Superman	Donovan	1966
Weekend	Eddie Cochran	1961
Monday Monday	Mamas and the Papas	1966
Friday on my Mind	Easybeats	1966
Yester-me Yester-you Yesterday	Stevie Wonder	1969
Nowhere to Run	Martha Reeves & Vandellas	1965
Love Me Do	The Beatles	1962
I Feel Fine	The Beatles	1964
From Me To You	The Beatles	1963

If you'd like to communicate with the author

or

if you want to buy another book

visit

www.agiftforanidiot.com

or

drop us a line at

DIRECTA (UK) LTD
Cold Norton, Essex. CM3 6UA
Ref:-Charity Book

Book will cost £7.50 including post & packing
Please make out cheques to
A gift for an Idiot...Charity Account
and don't forget to put in your name & address !